Kittens
KW-019

Contents

Origin—6
Your Kitten—22
Health Care—38
Grooming—60
Training—84
Index—93

Photographers: Blair Studio, Tom Caravaglia, Lewis Fineman, Manny Greenhaus, Florence M. Harrison, Heritage Studio, Dorothy Holby, Fritz Prenzel, Purina Pet Care Center, Ron Reagan, Kevin T. Sullivan, Sally Anne Thompson, Louise van der Meid, Joan Wastlhuber.

Front endpapers: A trio of adorable longhair kittens. **Title page:** Kittens have sweet expressions which make prospective owners fall in love with them on sight. **Back endpapers:** Kittens make wonderful pets for young and old people alike.

Distributed in the UNITED STATES by T.F.H. Publications, Inc., One T.F.H. Plaza, Neptune City, NJ 07753; in CANADA to the Pet Trade by H & L Pet Supplies Inc., 27 Kingston Crescent, Kitchener, Ontario N2B 2T6; Rolf C. Hagen Ltd., 3225 Sartelon Street, Montreal 382 Quebec; in CANADA to the Book Trade by Macmillan of Canada (A Division of Canada Publishing Corporation), 164 Commander Boulevard, Agincourt, Ontario M1S 3C7; in ENGLAND by T.F.H. Publications Limited, Cliveden House/Priors Way/Bray, Maidenhead, Berkshire SL6 2HP, England; in AUSTRALIA AND THE SOUTH PACIFIC by T.F.H. (Australia) Pty. Ltd., Box 149, Brookvale 2100 N.S.W., Australia; in NEW ZEALAND by Ross Haines & Son, Ltd., 18 Monmouth Street, Grey Lynn, Auckland 2, New Zealand; in SINGAPORE AND MALAYSIA by MPH Distributors (S) Pte., Ltd., 601 Sims Drive, #03/07/21, Singapore 1438; in the PHILIPPINES by Bio-Research, 5 Lippay Street, San Lorenzo Village, Makati Rizal; in SOUTH AFRICA by Multipet Pty. Ltd., 30 Turners Avenue, Durban 4001. Published by T.F.H. Publications, Inc. Manufactured in the United States of America by T.F.H. Publications, Inc.

KITTENS

KAY RAGLAND

Above: *Though independent creatures, feral cats are known to gather together in colonies; in the wild, certain big cats remain in families or prides until the youngsters are several years old.* **Right:** *An air of mystery and magic has accompanied the cat throughout the ages.*

Origins

While the origin of the domestic cat as pet is shrouded in antiquity, much as the roots of today's modern breeds of dogs are, evidence has been found that generally indicates that the cat has been intermingling with the modern civilizations of the day for roughly 30 centuries.

Remains from ancient Egyptian civilizations have given us the strongest case for the cat being a revered part of family life, and in this instance royal family life, centuries ago. When scientists entered the tombs of the pharaohs to gain information on a way of life modern man had no

previous access to, they found mummified cats buried in the innermost rooms of the pyramids along with other valuables most treasured by, and therefore buried with, the pharaohs. They also found hieroglyphics inscribed on the walls telling about a breed of cat that was held in high esteem.

There were times in the history of a number of countries in which magical and, in some cases, evil powers were attributed to the cat. It was persecuted and tortured mercilessly for supposed bewitching acts when these beliefs were prevalent. In many other societies, however, much the opposite has been true.

Some civilizations regarded the cat as a religious symbol and revered it highly as such. Certain countries consider the cat to

These Siamese kittens are proving that kittens love to get into mischief.

Although cats have been domesticated for years, some wild instincts still remain. These kittens are stalking. Through such "wild" behavior, they are learning about the world around them.

bring good fortune and one or a pair of cats are often given as a wedding present to bring fortune and prosperity to the newly married couple. In ancient societies, the cat was owned only by royalty and looked upon as a protector of the royal family.

There are legends and tales attempting to track down the origins of the cat. Many of these are plausible, but most of them simply cannot be proven one way or the other. Through art and logical deduction, the presence of cats can be found in China and Thailand (ancient Siam), though no conclusive proof exists for this. A rabbit living in that area today is the same color as our present day Siamese cat. Because of this many people think the Siamese came from that area as well, but this certainly does not settle the matter and no really conclusive proof exists that points to the Siamese cat being originally a native of Siam. Some writings, not always factual, have it that the Siamese cat was trained by royal families to guard the palace walls. Again, while evidence is sketchy, judging from the

Above: *The wild cat, a variety of lynx, is usually smaller than other members of the lynx family and is frequently found to mate with the domestic housecat. This does not mean, however, that the wild cat is easily domesticated.* **Opposite, upper left:** *It is not uncommon to find the ocelot, a small wild cat, kept as a pet.* **Opposite, upper right:** *The bobcat is the only variety of lynx found primarily in North America and northern Mexico.* **Opposite, bottom:** *The Northern Lynx lives in the northern forests of Europe, Asia, and North America.*

breed's attitude and strong sense of loyalty, together with its aggressive and outspoken nature, it is not too far fetched to imagine this breed serving in the capacity of a guard cat.

Cats of all types, large and small, domesticated and wild, are also believed to have lived in Mongolia during the time of Genghis Khan. Since there was very little set down in writing, not much is known about their size, color or general structure. What is assumed about them is that because ponies, oxen and other domesticated animals kept by the Monogolians in the northern areas of that country had heavy coats to fend off the cold climate, then the cats must also have developed a heavy coat of fur. Since it is known that the climate in southern Mongolia was milder, we assume that short hair cats probably developed there. Many sources believe that a cat similar to the modern Siamese cat came from this southern section of the

A tabby shorthair kitten roaming in the great outdoors.

A basket of Siamese kittens, progeny of a ten-month-old mother. Siamese cats mature earlier than cats of most other breeds.

Above: *The ocelot, a species of wild cat, lends itself readily to domestication. Though two to three times larger than the average housecat, it is still small enough to be kept as a pet by the more venturesome animal lover.* **Opposite:** *The Amur Leopard lives farther north than any other of the species, reaching into the Amur region of the Soviet Union.*

country, as did one that could have been the prototype of the present day Burmese.

So much for historical beginnings. Looking at genealogical beginnings (that is, at the animals that were related to the present day animal and probably responsible for shaping it into the particular type of animal it is today), our modern cat is believed to be descended from a weasel-like carnivore, Miacis, also believed to be a common ancestor to the dog. Cats probably came from Miacis by way of the civet, and appeared approximately 10 million years after Miacis had vanished from the scene. This being so, cats close to their present day appearance probably came on the scene 10 to 20 million years before dogs.

A kindle of beautiful Russian Blue kittens: Gr. Ch. Tsar Blue's Chip o'Willy, Gr. Ch. Tsar Blu's Flash of Sereshka, Ch. Tsar Blue's Moorka, and Ch. Tsar Blue's Silver Sonnet. Bred by Donna Fuller.

Shorthair kittens, a bicolor and a tabby.

In earliest times after cats evolved they divided into two groups: *Dinictis* and *Hoplophoneus*. Descendants of *Hoplophoneus*, best-known of which was the saber-toothed tiger, died out. Offspring of *Dinictis*, however, remained strong and flourished. It was from this branch of early cats that our modern cat derived almost without change. His litheness, intelligence, adaptable nature, physical strength and teeth, which were particularly good at tearing and stabbing, enabled Dinictis' decendants to keep pace with evolutionary times while certain other species died out. As one expert associated with the American Museum of Natural History sums up the tenacity of modern day cat: "Of all land-living carnivores, the cats are among the most completely specialized for a life of killing and for eating meat. They are very muscular, alert, supple carnivores, fully equipped for springing upon and destroying animals as large as or larger than themselves..."

Opposite: *The play of very young kittens encompasses many of the techniques they would use in stalking prey or existing in an outdoor environment.* **Above:** *Fresh air and sunshine are good for the new family. While the kittens are still very young, however, they should not be left unattended, even when they are with the mother cat.*

The cat's teeth, specialized for specific functions, made him a particularly efficient predator. Further attributes particularly notable in cats that have also remained unchanged to the present day are that smaller cats will take deftly to the trees while the larger cats remain chiefly earth-bound.

Although taxonomists differ as to which groups of animals should properly be known by which labels, we will use *Felis* to mean that group of cats that includes our modern domestic housecat, as well as some other small wild cats that are occasionally tamed. These are the puma or cougar, the golden cats, the jaguarundi, the ocelot, the margay, serval, lynx and bobcat. Most normally found in wilderness areas, these cats have been forced closer to man's habitat than they once were because of the encroachment of construction and commerce upon their lands. In fact, the puma has been seen in unexpected places in recent years. In 1958, a college professor reported seeing a puma on the shoulder of the Garden State Parkway near Long Branch, New Jersey.

The golden cats, other members of the group *Felis*, are found in Asia and west Africa. Both are about the size of a leopard and are a tawny yellow color. The serval is a "doggy" cat with long legs that runs down its prey on the open plains of equatorial Africa. Ranging from south-western United States to southern Chile, the jaguarundi takes in several varieties of closely related cats that appear more weasel-like than feline. They have long bodies and tails, short legs and small heads.

Also a member of *Felis*, the lynx is distinctive in appearance, with hind legs much longer than its forelegs. It has a stubby tail and broad paws, extremely long ear tufts and full facial whiskers that puff out like mutton-chop sideburns. The lynx, known for its intelligence, is found usually no further south than the Canadian border and in northern Europe and Asia.

The bobcat is a variety of lynx that is found mainly in America, southern Canada and northern Mexico. The caracal, another member of the lynx family, has slender long ears and is reddish brown in color. Its ears are tufted like its lynx cousin but it does not have the characteristic lynx mutton chops. The caracal, which has an extraordinarily powerful jump, is often kept as a pet in its native India.

Two more members of *Felis* are the ocelot and the margay, the smallest wild members of this group. The margay is about the size of a housecat, while the

Young kittens will get into anything within their reach. It is important, therefore, that a careful eye be kept on them.

ocelot is a little more than twice as large, ranging from 20 to 26 pounds in weight. Both are suitable as pets, but it must be remembered that the larger cat is also stronger and when it decides to sharpen its claws on your sofa, the damage done will be quite a bit more extensive than that done by your domestic puss.

Above: *The best time to obtain a kitten is after it has been thoroughly weaned and before it becomes too accustomed to its place of birth. The age of eight weeks is appropriate for most kittens.* **Right:** *If you want a kitten primarily for a pet, then you need not be concerned with its pedigree or lack thereof. The main ingredient in transforming a kitten into a pet is the care and attention you give it.*

Your Kitten

To obtain a kitten can be a relatively easy matter, but what a world of delight and companionship the addition to your home of that wee bundle of fur can be. You will find your kitten to be not only a pet, but a clown, an acrobat, a stalking tiger and at times a sleepy bundle that will seek out your lap when it is tired of moping and purr in utter contentment when she has found it—such is our charming friend, the kitten.

If you are seeking a kitten strictly as a pet, then it will not matter whether it is a pedigreed or stray, as long as it is healthy

and of good disposition. Whether the pet kitten you get is a male or female is strictly a matter of choice; both make good pets, though the males tend to range farther away from home as adults. As a responsible pet owner, however, who does not want to overpopulate the world with more cats than there are people to properly care for them, you can have either the male or female cat neutered through a relatively simple operation.

The color of the kitten may be a criterion for choice of pet, since a great many types of cats enjoy an extensive color range from tabby stripes in colors varying from cream through reds, rusts, browns, chestnuts, through gray to white and black, or various combinations of these colors. A few breeds are pointed, as the Siamese, having muzzle, tail tip and paws a solid color other than the solid ground color of its body.

Length of hair, whether short or long, may be another criterion

Kittens should get sufficient amounts of fresh air and sunshine, but be sure that they do not nibble on any poisonous plants.

Kittens come in many adorable colors and patterns. Note the white on the paws and chest of this marmalade-colored kitten.

upon which to base your choice. Though kittens are all mainly individuals when it comes to personality, certain patterns of personality do tend to accompany longhairs that differ from those of shorthairs. The same also tends to be true of certain colors of cats, as well as different breeds. For example, the Siamese is among the better known for possessing a very aggressive, verbose, though loving if somewhat possessive personality.

Handling The Kitten

A kitten should never be picked

Above: *Most older cats will be tolerant of a kitten as long as the two have been properly introduced.* **Opposite, upper left:** *The tortoiseshell markings on this kitten are almost exclusively found in female cats.* **Opposite, upper right:** *This longhair kitten shares its red tabby coloring with its shorthair cousins.* **Opposite, bottom:** *White is a dominant color in domestic shorthair cats.*

Five-week-old Abyssinian kittens owned by Joan and Alfred Wastlhuber, Nepenthes Cattery. Abyssinians are among the most popular purebred cats.

up by the scruff of the neck. "But the mother cat carries her babies that way," you say. Sure she does, but she is carrying a very tiny baby with very little body weight. Within a short time, the kitten's body becomes too heavy for this handling and to put the entire strain of the heavier body on the skin of the neck could be injurious.

The correct way to pick up the kitten is to place one hand under the hind feet and the other under the body just behind the front feet. Or, you can put one hand across the rear of the body with the tail curled under, and the other hand between the front feet. Don't drop a kitten suddenly or from any distance. If you have to put her down, put her down directly on the floor or on whatever object you wish. What is a small distance to us is a long distance to the kitten. As she grows, she can ably take more distance.

Beds and Furnishings

Some kittens like a cat bed and others prefer various spots. The house cat will enjoy a sunny window ledge during the day and may sleep on the bed with you at night, if you allow it. He can be easily trained to relax on a sheet of newspaper on a certain chair or chairs and once he acquires this habit, he will seek out the paper and not jump on the furniture at random. Most cats like to seek out high places to sleep, the higher the better.

Bookcases, mantels, and shelves all fascinate them. During the colder weather they will seek out the warmth of the television set or even radios.

A friend of mine with three Siamese cats purchased a home which had huge rafters in the front room. These rafters delighted the cats, who spent most of their time on them, leaping from one to the other with ease. This, however, was a little disconcerting to visitors, as the sight of not one but three

Owning a pair of kittens is twice as fun as owning one. Kittens of the same age, when raised together, will usually become great friends.

Opposite: *While cats are reputed to have an extraordinary sense of balance, they are not incapable of taking a tumble. Cats that have fallen from extreme heights have been known to sustain serious head injuries, and some of these injuries can be fatal.* **Above:** *The kittens and cats pictured here are all pedigreed. Some, like the Persian (bottom left), are very old breeds, while others, like the Ragdoll (center left), have only been developed within the last several years. Still others, like the Maine Coon (bottom right), are believed to be indigenous only to a specific area.*

cats leaping across the room on rafters quite a distance apart certainly startled them.

The cat bed is somewhat like the dog bed but usually has a sort of hooded top. Conventional cushions with washable covers complete the bed. Any wicker basket or even the plastic type may be used.

Kittens cannot resist a small box like a shoe box. They will climb in, turn around and around, and no matter the size, the cat will fold into the box. Perhaps a paw and the tail may get left out, but the cat is in. A sheet of tissue paper in the box will entice her into complete relaxation for hours.

About the only furnishings for a cat would be a collar or harness with leash. They can be taught easily to walk on a public street with the harness and leash, as well as to ride in cars. My neighbor has a beautiful black long haired cat with a

Below: *Persian kittens.* **Opposite:** *Kittens have the ability to find toys wherever they go.*

round white spot right in the middle of his tummy. "Snowball" has to have his nightly walk and run, so every evening on goes his harness and extra long leash and down the street he goes, towing behind him the man of the family. First Snowball runs several house lengths, turns and heads back towards his home. This goes on several times, then he settles down and briskly sets out down the street, enjoying the smells around the trees, paying no attention whatsoever to any passer-by. Together they walk to the very end of the street where he turns by himself and walks his master back home.

Getting your kitten to wear a harness makes traveling with him easier, as it is then unnecessary to put him in a cat traveling cage, at least not all the time. You must always keep him under control and prevent him leaping from the car should he be frightened.

A group of playful kittens pouncing on Christmas ornaments.

Yes, kittens are even capable of getting into jewelry boxes!

The standard cat collar is made with a flexible length of some rubberized material which will allow the cat to get free should he catch the collar on a fence, tree limb or any other obstruction. If your cat is free to roam, make him wear a collar outdoors with an identification tag on it, just in case a well-meaning neighbor should pick your cat up thinking he is a stray in need of a home. The ribbon or conventional collar, that is so attractive on your cat while he is in the house, could well be a death trap outdoors, strangling your pet to death should he become tangled in brambles or caught on some other projection that he cannot free himself from.

There are cat coats and bootees to be had, but I doubt the cat takes kindly to them. Every cat I have seen so dressed wears a very embarrassed look, but it is probably that I am prejudiced against decorating any animal. In the winter a house cat should have a coat or sweater when it is taken outside.

Toys

Anything that moves, rustles or sways is a toy for the kitten—bits of paper, small lengths of string, a paperclip, a button, the leaves of your best plant and a dripping faucet. Puss spends hours catching the drip from the faucet and each drop seems to startle him over and over. Tie a wad of paper to a string and hang it over the rung of a chair or get him a ping pong ball to bat around and chase. There is nothing that won't attract his attention, and he makes games out of impossible objects.

Catnip toys can prove a source of exercise as well as amusement as the catnip causes puss to go on a catnip binge with resultant frolicking, rolling and biting the toy. In addition to the mouse shape, you can get catnip balls, catnip bones and numerous other forms.

All small balls of rubber, string, or plastic will give him hours of amusement. Try tossing him three ping pong balls at once and you will see some fast kitty-movement.

Possibly one of the most practical toys, if toy it can be called, is the scratching pole. This is a round or square piece of wood, about three inches in diameter, covered with a couple of layers of carpeting or heavy material, and placed upright on a platform arrangement. Puss is supposed to do his sharpening of claws and scratching on this pole and leave the legs of the furniture alone. Luckily, he easily gets the idea, and, when the urge to give his claws a work-out arrives, he will use this scratching pole.

Be sure to remove any items that pose a danger to your kitten or to which your kitten may pose a danger.

Health Care

A healthy kitten should be full of activity and should be interested in its surroundings.

Your love and attention are necessary items to your new kitten if he is to thrive and be happy. But all the love in the world will not keep him happy if he is lacking nutritionally, or if his other health needs have been overlooked. Some people think that because felines give the impression of independence they need little or no looking after. This is far from the truth. Keeping the domestic cat in conditions that are most convenient for his human companions often means that he cannot pursue the activities that are natural to him and must give up much of the physical exercise that goes along with them. Nor does the house cat eat the same types of food he would if he were fending for himself in the great outdoors. He must eat the commercial preparations that are served for him. Not all of these contain all the ingredients of a balanced diet, necessary for his good health. Sometimes a strictly canned diet, in combination with his relatively easy living conditions, causes him to fall prey to some diseases and ailments that his more independent, outdoor relatives may not. For these reasons, cat owners must pay close attention to their felines' diet, methods of sanitation and other circumstances of his environment for which he is primarily dependent upon his humans to supply.

Feeding

By one means or another, you now have a kitten, purring one moment and giving out tiny hisses the next at some imagined fright. Your problem is—how to care for such a creature?

A nutritious, well-balanced diet will go a long way in keeping your kitten healthy and fit.

Kittens can readily adapt themselves to any condition. It only takes a bit of knowledge and any person can have an adorable kitten which will turn into a beguiling pet, a pet that is full of dignity and charm. As you talk to her, the eyes will close to a mere slit, the end of her tail will sway to and fro, and a sense of companionship will develop between you that can never be destroyed.

But what to properly feed the

Note the beautiful coats and the bright eyes of these Siamese kittens. These two factors indicate good health.

A bicolored shorthair kitten.

newcomer? It's very easy, especially if you start the kitten off right, giving her a variety of foods. Milk, to be sure, is a staple item but should always be given at room temperature or a little warmer—never cold from the refrigerator. You can use fresh milk or evaporated milk, diluted or full strength, the amount to vary depending upon the size of the kitten. As a start, try about two teaspoonsful, then gradually increase the amount. It is not wise to leave milk on the floor too long as it might sour and pick up bits of dust and dirt. A cat, being a fastidious creature, enjoys clean food in clean dishes.

Start the kitten off on scraped beef for the first solid food. This is done by using a blunt bread knife and running it over a bit of raw beef. The residue on the knife is soft. Place this on the end of your finger and wave it under the kitten's nose. She may

A tabby shorthair kitten. Exercise is a must for a growing kitten.

not take it, but if you rub it across her lips she will lick it off. Or, you may insert it at the side of her mouth. Remember to keep the amount very small to avoid choking her. You can add scraped liver and baby food for variety. As she learns to eat, the meat can be chopped into small bits. Again—no ice-cold foods.

As the kitten gains in size and weight, her diet should consist of meats, liver, heart, brains, chicken and fish, both raw and cooked, most of which are available in commercially prepared canned foods. Pork is not good except as an occasional meal. When your kitten is 8 weeks old, it is no longer necessary to chop up the food in small bits. The cat is a carnivorous animal with sharp fangs to tear and rip meat into pieces.

It is well to give a variety of foods to prevent your kitten from becoming choosy and refusing many of the foods that provide a balanced diet.

All cats like fish and chicken. Great care must be taken to remove all fish bones when feeding fresh fish. Raw or cooked are both acceptable, and a part of a can of sardines with the oil will be relished with much lip-licking. Chicken bones are never to be given, as a swallowed splinter would be a serious matter. Chicken skin, rejected portions, heart and any other organ make an excellent change.

Dry cat foods are valuable at times and can be used mixed with the regular food, soaked in milk or broth, or even used dry.

Always be sure to feed sufficient amounts of food for each kitten. Sometimes a larger kitten will bully its smaller friends, who will not get enough to eat because of him.

A well-fed kitten will have boundless energy and a zest for living. His activities will entertain its owner for hours.

Some canned cat foods have a certain amount of liquid. Use a portion of dry food and pour the liquid from the canned food over it. When the dry food has absorbed all the liquid, empty the rest of the can into it and thoroughly mix. This provides a more solid food for your young cat. A mixing of this kind will make two good meals for one cat.

Most cats like vegetables, especially the green ones. I had one cat that would come running every time I opened a can of string beans, and she would eat as much as I would give her. She also like asparagus, spinach, peas, and, of all things, lettuce. In addition to the vegetables, she greatly relished the liquid that accompanied the canned vegetables, and I always saved her a portion. Cooked carrots often will be eaten. Try out the cat on whatever vegetable you have and you will be surprised how many she will consume...but it's a *very* expensive diet! Canned cat foods are much more inexpensive and practical.

When kittens and cats are a little off their feed, they will seek out grass which they will chew and swallow, then, with a gulping motion empty their stomachs—a procedure which seems to relieve them. Ordinarily, however, they eat grass only when they seem to have a special need for it.

When no grass or vegetable is provided, you may find the cat chewing on your house plant. So, should you notice Puss eyeing your best fern or philodendron, or tentatively testing out your prize geranium, better get her to

Persian and other longhair kittens will need ample grooming in order to keep their coats in good condition.

the kitchen and offer her something in the vegetable family, even if it's only a few blades of grass. Better still, have a 'cat garden' either in the house or outside. The house garden consists of a large pot with a few catnip toys and a small amount of grass. When the catnip toys get chewed up, replace them.

One summer I decided to put in an outdoor garden for quick growing so I planted a space about four feet square. The catnip came up beautifully—and so did all the neighborhood cats. One morning I found all sizes and kinds of cats, rolling and chewing on the catnip which had been reduced to stumps. To this day I have never seen a happier bunch of cats.

When your kitten is hungry, you will certainly know it as she will stalk around the kitchen, meowing loudly. Should you be in another room of the house, she will come to you, then run back toward the kitchen as if trying to lead you to the food.

Every kitten is an individual, and each will have its own particular likes and dislikes. As you get to know your kitten, you will learn what its particular favorites are.

A tabby and white shorthair kitten. A kitten should be given some vegetables in its diet, but be sure that it does not fill this need by munching on any dangerous plants.

Grown cats should be fed twice a day, with milk available in between. The kitten should be fed more often, but a full grown cat is usually satisfied with one heavy meal a day and one a little lighter.

One cat I had was a fussy eater. He liked liver best of all and would eat it very heartily.

Foolishly, he was given liver day after day, usually with other foods which he discarded. Then I found he would touch nothing but liver which, in itself, would have been all right (though terribly expensive) but there were times I was unable to get to the store and ran out of liver—hence a hungry and very

47

annoyed cat. To avoid this problem start the cat off eating different foods and change the food often to prevent a one-food cat.

Some cats require more food than others, and often the heartiest eater is the rangiest cat, while the fussy eater will be plump and rounded. One meal a day should be larger than the other, yet if the cat leaves any appreciable amount, cut down next time. You will soon discover an amount that will satisfy the cat's appetite with no left-overs.

Should the kitten refuse food, take the food away and make no more attempts to feed him for a few hours. If he still refuses it, don't worry. However, should he refuse food the second day, it is possible he may have a hairball or the beginning stages of some

A sealpoint Siamese kitten. Siamese cats tend to be a bit louder than cats of other breeds, but they are also considered more attentive to their owners.

A sable Burmese kitten. A purebred kitten will be more expensive than a pet quality kitten.

other ailment.

Housebreaking

When you get the kitten, you must determine if he is to be a house cat (that is, kept in the house entirely), or a cat allowed to be outside part of the time. Persons living in cities, especially apartments, are often unable to

allow the cat outside freedom so they have to provide a litter box.

If your cat will be free to come and go at will, he will still have to be taught that his duties must be done outside. The kitten may be too small when you first get him to allow him to go outside, so provide a small box containing litter, available at your pet shop or grocery, and every so often take him to the box and place him it. With his paws, gently dig a little hole. Nature taught the cat to cover up his waste, so this habit is inherent in the kitten. Keep the box always available and on sheets of paper. The box should not be too high for him to

Cats are naturally clean animals. Expect your kitten to give itself a good grooming after coming in after a romp outside.

climb into by himself. Then as he gets larger, take both the kitten and the box outside and leave the box. Then whenever he is in the house and you notice him going to where the box was kept, pick him up and take him outside to the box. In a few days he will

go to the door himself and ask to be let out. Keep in mind that the kitten is bound to make a few mistakes and if you leave him for any long period of time in the house, you are sure to regret it. Remember, he is only a baby and as yet knows no better.

To make it easier for the cat to go in and out without your having to open the door each time, have a small door cut in your back door, replacing the cut piece by means of a hinge at the top which will allow the cat to push it either way. This opening will be much too small for anything but the cat to enter. Be sure that the replaced bit of wood is not tightly fitted or the cat can't move it.

Now for the indoor cat. This cat is going to use a cat pan for a long time so it is better not to use a make-shift affair. There are regular cat pans on the market, made of plastic about 20 x 16 inches. Or, you can obtain a white enamelled pan about 2 inches deep, 20 x 16 inches.

Many types of cat litters can be used. Any of the commercial cat litters are not only excellent but easily disposable and most contain a chemical, harmless to the cat, but which prevents odors. They are also very absorbent and quickly dried. The cat droppings are easily picked up by use of a cat rake and tray, purchased in any pet store, and disposed of by flushing down the

Be sure to begin training your kitten to use its litter box as soon as possible. If you don't, you may not like the place it chooses on its own.

toilet. The larger the size of litter you purchase, the less it will cost. A 5 pound bag costs about twice as much per pound as a 50 pound bag.

Sawdust comes next for easy disposal. To the sawdust, shavings can be added. The only objection to the sawdust is that it is picked up on the cat's paws and carried through the house. Sand and yard dirt can both be used but have to be changed more often as they retain the odor. Shredded paper is often used but it is messy.

Deep pans are not good nor are smaller ones. It is suggested that the cat pan be placed on several thicknesses of paper.

A shorthair ginger kitten and a longhair blue cream kitten.

White kittens may require more coat care than kittens of other colors since their coats are more likely to become stained.

Cats like to cover a used hole and in their diligence, may shove some of the litter out of the pan, or may, on occasion, miss the pan entirely although most of the body will be inside. The paper will catch the residue.

The pan should be entirely cleaned out and the litter thrown away, replaced with fresh litter, every 3 days. A good wash with hot water and soap will amply clean it. Do not use any of the coal tar derivatives or carbolic soaps, nor any of the strong disinfectants. If possible, after

Havana Brown kitten. Your kitten should have a place that it can call its own.

washing put the pan out in the sun.

Some cats make their own toilet arrangements such as using the bathtub. If this should occur, don't punish the cat but rather take him to the litter box. If he continues to prefer the tub fill it with a scant half inch of water, just enough to discourage him. Try to find out why he is refusing the cat pan, even if you have to move its location.

To show what an individual puss is, there is a cute story about a writer who brought home a kitten from the street, hungry and forlorn. Jerome, as the cat was named, was provided with all the luxuries including a fine cat pan which he refused to use. His choice was the writer's wastebasket. No matter where the wastebasket was put, Jerome followed. Finally in desperation, the writer bought a second wastebasket, put in the litter and showed it to Jerome. Around and around walked Jerome, then into the basket he hopped and performed his duty. Since that time Jerome is happy, the writer is very happy, and, best of all, the writer's wastebasket contains what it should—waste paper.

Ailments

One day you may notice puss retching and gulping and soon up will come a long mass resembling the stool of the animal. This is actually a hairball consisting of hair ingested from the cat's grooming. The fact that he has disgorged it is, in itself, good, as the condition at least is solved temporarily. Should the

Longhair silver chinchilla kittens owned by Adele Magill.

hairball not be dislodged through the mouth, it could go into the intestines and cause a lot of trouble or even remain in the stomach with the result that the cat would refuse to eat. Usually by this time, the cat would seek out grass to assist in relieving himself of the hairball.

Hairballs can be eliminated by the constant grooming of the cat with a good comb and brush.

Scratching may mean two things—loose and dead hair which should be brushed away, or possibly worms or eczema. If your cat has worms, you will be able to detect them in his stool. Commercial worm medicines are available on the market that can be mixed with your pet's food to rid him of these pests. They are safe and effective; however, instructions on the box should

A kitten's coat is its crowning glory. Therefore, regular grooming is a must for good looks and for health.

A lovely Abyssinian kitten. Shorthair kittens are, in general, not as quick to get hairballs as are longhair kittens, but they must be groomed regularly in order to prevent hairballs from forming.

be read and followed conscientiously.

Fleas are easily detected by parting the cat's fur in the areas beneath the arm pits or under the chin. Constant combing will keep down this pest and remove most of the eggs, but should you one day discover a full crop of both fleas and eggs, use a good cat flea powder and sprinkle the back of his neck (where he cannot lick it off). Sprinkle also

crevices around his bed and sleeping places, then cover the bed or whatever pillow he may use with another piece of cloth.

Constipation is another ailment of the cat usually caused by the lack of greens or vegetables, too rich a diet, or even too many cooked foods. The restricted house cat will strain while in her box of sand and you can readily ascertain this condition. A meal of fresh

Knowing your kitten is the best way for you to react quickly when something is wrong with it. The faster your kitten is treated, the more likely it is to recover.

liver, plenty of vegetables, a few drops of mineral oil in the milk, or even dropped by means of an eye-dropper into the *sides* of the mouth will relieve the ailment. Never give a cat medicine from the front as it may cause him to choke. Also never place his head back and force down any medicines, liquid or pills.

Diarrhea demands the opposite type of treatment—no meats, vegetables, or even milk, unless he will take buttermilk. Instead give him egg white, a bit of bread with egg yolk or cheese. Most cats like cheese and usually, some finely chopped mild cheese will cure this ailment.

Not only are most cat ailments rare, but they are difficult to diagnose and cure. If your cat is listless or acts abnormally, take him to your local veterinarian.

Opposite: *A lovely female Scottish Fold kitten, Beachmor Jessica, bred and owned by Mr. and Mrs. F.M. Dreifuss.*

Grooming

Good grooming is recommended for any cat whether it is to be a show cat or strictly a pet. To a certain extent, the grooming required for a pet cat will be somewhat less than for a show cat, yet for either one regular grooming will be a healthy stimulant for coat and skin. If your new kitten is a

Indoor cats do not need grooming as often as outdoor cats, but do not neglect their coats.

longhair, then your job is going to take a little longer, but not much.

The first step toward a healthy coat is a good diet. Cats that are suffering from poor nutrition will not have the lustrous, rich coat that is natural to a cat. So too, a cat that is continually fighting off many minor ailments will not have a healthy looking coat. The tools needed for grooming your kitten are quite simple—a hard rubber brush, like the curry comb used on horses and dogs, and a fine-toothed comb. Because of the texture of a cat's hair, a coarse-toothed comb will not be very effective. Before using any grooming tools, inspect the coat and try to loosen dead hairs from your kitten's coat so that they will be easier to brush out. A good way to do this is to moisten your fingertips and work them through your cat's coat against the lay of the coat. You are actually giving your pet a massage, going right down to the skin, for this is the best way not to miss any loose or dead hairs. Gently bring your hands, with fingers parted, from the roots up through the hairs to their tips. Now that the dead hairs have been brought to the surface, the curry comb and fine-toothed steel comb will be most efficient for removing them.

Aside from keeping your cat

A pair of tabby and white shorthair kittens.

looking his best, frequent grooming is a preventive measure against hairballs that build up in your cat's stomach. While most cats normally can spit these up without a serious problem, it is not unusual for these hairballs to cause constipation, severe vomiting and other problems when they become lodged in the cat's intestines or throat and he is unable to rid himself of them. In longhair cats, the hairball problem can be worse. Several commercial products on the market tend to lessen the problem by aiding in the elimination of accumulated hair.

Matting of hair is a grooming problem that tends to occur more frequently in longhair cats than in short hairs. The degree of knotting, or matting, has a great

A pair of young Abyssinian littermates.

A shaded silver American Shorthair kitten from the Frosticat Cattery.

deal to do with the texture and length of hair of the individual coat. Fine hair mats more readily than coarse hair.

To untangle a mat, begin with your fingers. Work the mat apart as much as possible with your fingertips, always remembering to be as gentle as possible. At the other end of the hair, a kitten is attached! If you cannot get the mat altogether out with your fingers, you can use a seam ripper, a small hand tool used by seamstresses, to finish taking the smaller mats out. While this tool works excellently, it still must be used very carefully to avoid hurting your cat, or tearing the hair and ruining the coat. This is especially important if your pet is a show cat. The seam ripper, available at stores that specialize in sewing supplies, has a little U-shaped blade inserted into a handle. Insert the seam ripper at the base of the

A mother cat will groom her kittens until they are old enough to leave her.

knot, lifting the blade up and out. The blade frees the fragile hair without discomfort to the cat and without removing great chunks of the coat. If you don't have a seam ripper, the last one or two teeth of a steel comb works almost as well. Insert these in the same manner as a seam ripper, lifting them gently toward

the tips of the hair. Under no circumstances should you put the whole comb at the base of a large knot and try to pull it all out at once. It is very painful to your cat and will probably make him leery of ever allowing you to groom him again. It also results in large hunks of hair being completely removed from the cat's coat. What would be left after such a method of dematting would definitely not be a show coat.

Stud Tail
Stud tail or grease tail is the result of overactive glands at the base of the tail and along the top of the tail. These glands secrete a heavy, dark grease or waxlike substance. Stud tail occurs in cats of all ages and both sexes, although breeding males seem to be afflicted with it more than neutered males and female cats.

To groom a cat with stud tail, cleanse the affected area with a mild detergent—emphasis on "mild." Wash the area repeatedly with warm water, scrubbing the detergent right down to the skin by using a small round shoe polish brush or a toothbrush. Be careful to confine the scrubbing to the area that is affected, since such intensive scrubbing with soap will dry out the normal hair. Allow the soap to remain on the skin a few minutes, if the cat will permit it, then rinse well. Keep repeating

Train your kitten or kittens to accept grooming as part of the regular routine. Begin getting them used to grooming at as early an age as possible.

Above: *Most cats develop a sense of height at a fairly early age. If your pet likes sitting at a window sill, you can usually trust its instincts to keep it from jumping from a height that is too high for it to manage.* **Opposite, upper left:** *Kittens give evidence of their gameness at a very early age.* **Opposite, upper right:** *These two kittens, though very young, are caught up in the adventure of stalking prey, be it a leaf, bug, or something else.* **Opposite, bottom:** *As your kitten matures, it will take on an air of majesty and serenity.*

Grooming

the process until the hair is squeaky clean. In severe cases where the skin has become raw because of the condition, Surgeon's Soap or a soap recommended by your veterinarian should be used instead of a plain detergent. Towel dry and put boric acid powder on the area while the hair is still damp. Work the powder well down into the hair next to the skin.

Nail Clipping

Nail clipping is essential for all cats. It should be started in kittenhood and continued at regular intervals throughout the year. Special cat nail clippers can be purchased at any pet shop.

For "at home" cats, only the front paws need be clipped, but for show cats all four feet should have the nails trimmed regularly. Grasp the foot in one hand,

A shorthair tabby cat with her three kittens. If you plan to show your cat in pedigree or family pet classes, it must be groomed to perfection.

A longhair ginger kitten and a longhair cream kitten.

gently applying pressure on the middle of the foot with thumb and forefinger to extend the complete length of the claws. Only the transparent tip of the claw should be removed. To prevent splintering and splitting of the claw, clippers should be held sideways so that they cut from both sides of the nail,

Opposite: Longhair kittens take longer to groom than shorthairs, but there is nothing like a beautiful, long, flowing coat. **Above:** If yours is a kitten that always seems to get into mischief, keeping it looking neat may be a bit of a chore—a chore that is well worth the effort in the long run.

rather than from top to bottom. Avoid clipping too far down on the nail, as you will hit the quick, causing intense pain to your cat and a possible infection.

Ear Care

Most cats clean their ears quite admirably all by themselves. However, when it does become necessary to clean their ears, the ear cleaning operation should present no problem in normally healthy cats. Use a cotton-tipped bendable stick and dip it in warm water and a mild soap, (such as Johnson's Baby Soap or Neutrogena). Rub the cotton-tipped applicator lightly over the inner ear surfaces, taking care not to drip water or probe too deeply into the ear.

Digging or scratching at the ear indicates the possibility of ear mites. Visit your veterinarian immediately if you suspect this, as the condition can worsen rapidly.

A kitten has excellent hearing which should remain with it for the rest of its life.

An adorable ginger kitten. Good grooming will help your kitten lead a long, happy life.

Dental Care

While a cat fed on a diet of good quality commercially prepared food should have clean, bright teeth and pink healthy gums, it won't hurt to check them from time to time. If you notice a tartar build up, a trip to the vet is in order. Instruments can be purchased for scaling your cat's teeth, but this is not advisable and should be left to the experienced, steady hand of your veterinarian.

Opposite, top: *The coat of lighter colored cats and kittens will sometimes show soiling more readily than that of darker colored coats, especially if they spend much time outdoors.* **Opposite, bottom:** *The domestic cat that is well cared for always seems to have a neat appearance.* **Right:** *If you wish to keep your longhair kitten looking glamorous with a minimum of effort, visit your pet shop and try some of the powders and dry bath treatments available.*

Crunchy dry food or occasional chunks of raw beef will reduce tartar formation on the teeth and provide exercise for the gums as well. Unpleasant breath odors are usually an indication that all is not well. They may mean dirty teeth, improper diet or a sickly condition that has not yet become noticeable through other symptoms.

A shorthair ginger kitten and a longhair cream kitten.

A tabby and white longhair kitten. Do not bathe your kitten too often, as this can dry out the coat.

Bathing

Bathing your cat can be an easy operation, keeping in mind the bywords for dealing with cats: gentleness and patience. It is a good idea to accustom your cat to baths when he is still a kitten. While kittens and cats have a natural aversion to water, they can be conditioned to view it as a non-frightening experience if you approach the whole bath time situation resourcefully. Here is one approach to making your kitten feel secure while being bathed.

Take a sturdy piece of board just slightly more narrow than the width and somewhat longer than the length of the tub or sink you will use and cover it with a rug fastened in place. Place it on a slant in the tub filled with water so that the bottom end rests against the side of the tub, while the top of the board projects out over the opposite side. Put your cat on this at whatever level he

Above: *Some cats are so attached to their homes that they are content to view the outdoors through a window and have no desire to leave the house. Do not, however, give your indoor cat the opportunity to run outside through an inadvertently opened door.* **Opposite:** *Whether they remain indoors most of the time or go outside frequently, kittens are never at a loss for a new situation to explore.*

first seems comfortable with; you can raise or lower him easily as needed without ever taking support away from under his feet. If the cat can hold onto something, other than your arm, while he is being bathed, it should make the whole process more pleasant for both of you.

The temperature of the water should be lukewarm. Begin the bath by wetting his head first. Once his head is wet, your cat usually will not mind having the rest of his body wet. Beginning with his head serves a second purpose. If you are bathing him to rid him of fleas, the pests will not be able to take refuge in your pet's ears, eyes or mouth when you wet the rest of the body. Be sure not to use soaps, shampoos, or detergents made for human use.

Thorough rinsing is a must. Using a spray nozzle for the rinsing process is the most efficient way to insure your kitten's coat will be thoroughly rinsed of all soap residue. The water should be tepid, as in the soaping phase, and should be flowing only fast enough to put a light pressure on the cat; otherwise he may become frightened and try to run. Rinse repeatedly until you are sure every bit of soap is gone.

When you are ready for drying, be sure to have a quantity of towels on hand. Lift the cat or

kitten out of the water and into a towel. Wrap it and gently squeeze head, feet, tail, and body. Remove the towel and let the cat shake himself, then with a second clean, dry towel repeat the entire process. Put the cat into a carrier near a radiator or in a warm spot to let him groom himself. When he is partially dry, comb him through and replace him so he can continue licking himself dry. When thoroughly dried, comb and brush him one final time. A hair drier makes this whole drying-grooming process much simpler as you can groom him at the same time you are drying. However, if you use a hair drier on your kitten, make sure it is neither too hot nor too close to him so as to burn either his skin or coat.

Dry Hair

Extensive breaking of hairs can often be cured by using a good protein coat conditioner. A dull, dry and lifeless coat on a cat prevents the coat's proper growth. If the skin seems healthy, but your kitten's coat is still on the dry side, try a coat conditioner made especially for cats. Dry, flaky skin or rough scaly skin, and loss of hair should warn you that your kitten may have a serious problem. See your veterinarian as soon as possible. Coat conditioners are just that: they treat the cat's

A pair of Maine Coon kittens. Left is Schick's Kabuki, a brown mackerel tabby female owned by Melanie Robertson. Right is Ch. Schick's Shendorah Valentine, a tortoiseshell and white female owned by Sharyn and Richard Bass. Both kittens were bred by Sharyn and Richard Bass.

coat, but can do nothing for the source of the problem, if that problem is caused by inadequate diet, too much bathing that has removed natural body oils, or undiagnosed illness.

Coat Discoloration
You may notice a rusty discoloration on an older cat's coat, though it occurs most frequently in certain longhairs. This is usually caused by licking, overexposure to direct sunlight, dampness and certain food stains. It is found primarily on the bib, ruff and back of your cat. This reddish discoloring when

found in a cream colored cat is referred to as a "hot" or darkened coat. It is not permanent and the new coat, when it comes in, will carry no traces of the rusty discoloration.

Rusting, if it is really an annoyance or clouds your hopes of showing your new black kitten, can sometimes be lessened by rubbing Listerine on the area. Dampen a cotton wad in the undiluted solution, wipe the areas that are discolored and let them dry. Several applications, some days apart, are usually necessary before the discoloration goes away.

Training kittens and cats includes teaching them to stay off the furniture. If you don't wish to allow your kitten on the sofa, begin to teach this lesson as soon as possible.

Since 1952, *Tropical Fish Hobbyist* has been the source of accurate, up-to-the-minute, and fascinating information on every facet of the aquarium hobby. Join the more than 50,000 devoted readers world-wide who wouldn't miss a single issue.

THE WORLD'S LARGEST SELECTION OF PET AND ANIMAL BOOKS

T.F.H. Publications publishes more than 900 books covering many hobby aspects (dogs,

. . . BIRDS . .

. . CATS . . .

. . . ANIMALS . . .

. . . DOGS . .

. . FISH . . .

cats, birds, fish, small animals, etc.), plus books dealing with more purely scientific aspects of the animal world (such as books about fossils, corals, sea shells, whales and octopuses). Whether you are a beginner or an advanced hobbyist you will find exactly what you're looking for among our complete listing of books. For a free catalog fill out the form on the other side of this page and mail it today. All T.F.H. books are recyclable.

Getting a kitten's attention is the first step to teaching it tricks. Try to train one kitten at a time. This way, there is less possibility of distraction.

Use your kitten's likes and dislikes to your advantage when training. Almost all cats love to chase something that is dangled in front of them.

After you and your new kitten have gotten to know each other, and he has gotten used to his new surroundings, you may find that teaching your cat tricks is not only fun but an enjoyable way to enhance your friendship with your new pet. Your cat's playful nature plus his natural affection for anyone who treats him kindly make him a very apt student. You may be surprised to find that cats, under the right circumstances, love to perform!

If you have decided to teach your kitten tricks or commands, it is best to start when he has grown a bit older, at around nine months of age. Remember, in training a cat gentleness and patience are the key words.

Cats do not respond well to fear-training or training by force. A quiet, gentle approach reinforced always by rewards of food each time your cat has done what you want him to, whether he has done it by himself or with your gentle persuasion, is the most effective way and will eventually bring the results you want.

The food rewards should consist of his favorite treats. When you reward him, do so only when he has done the trick or obeyed the command correctly. If you reward him for doing it the wrong way then you will be reinforcing what you don't want him to do. However, part of enabling him to do the trick correctly is giving him consistently simple commands. Use the same one for the same trick each time you practice it. Do not make the command overly wordy, or change the way you express the command from one time to the next. Also, do not allow any time to lapse before giving him the food treat, otherwise he will not associate

Opposite: *A pair of longhair ginger kittens.*

Above: *Teaching your cat to jump through a hoop is not as difficult as it may seem. It must be done in two different steps, but after your pet has mastered each one, it will soon perform the whole procedure with one command.* **Opposite:** *The natural agility of kittens makes them good candidates for trick training.*

the treat with complying with your command.

At the outset of training, a good way to start is with five minute training sessions followed by half hour rest periods. Continue alternating the training intervals with the rest breaks until you have reached a total of 20 or 25 minutes of training. As you work with your cat more, you will be better able to judge his capacity for length of training sessions and how long he can continue on any given day.

Here are some commands and tricks it would be practical for your cat to know as well as some that are just plain "cute." These are the ones that really show off your training abilities and his I.Q. The first one is the "sit here." Begin this trick or command by rubbing a little food on your finger and letting your cat smell it. Then place a tidbit of food on the floor a little way from him, tap the spot on the floor where the food is and say "sit here." When he has come to that spot for the food, repeat the procedure, moving to another position. Do this over several times, each time saying "sit here." Your cat will soon get the idea. To make sure he sits when he has come to the spot you have indicated, gently push his hindquarters down into a sitting position. After a while, you will

find that you no longer have to tap the floor, but can merely point to the spot you want your cat to sit, and he will understand what is expected of him.

The next procedure can be used to train your cat to stay indoors or out of a particular room you do not wish him to enter. Unlike most others, this procedure does not require the use of a food reward. Leave the door to the room you do not want him in slightly ajar, wide enough to arouse his curiosity, but not wide enough for him to go through. As he approaches the open door, take a folded newspaper and swat the floor or wall near the door several times, not hard enough to frighten him to death but just enough to make him apprehensive to want to come through. Repeat the procedure as often as needed until the cat no longer shows any desire to investigate that particular room.

You may transfer the paper swatting activity to the doors leading outside to train him to stay inside, though it may take a little longer since the smells and sounds from outside will act as a greater motivator than the cat's normal curiosity.

The next set of tricks can be considered really that—tricks, rather than useful commands. These are the ones that show off both you and your cat's talents.

No trick involving high jumps should be taught until the kitten's body is mature enough. In addition, never train your cat to perform a dangerous trick.

Some tricks make use of a natural instinct. The "retrieve" is one of these. Watch your cat for a time when he is engaging in one of the many play sessions cats frequently become caught up in to amuse themselves. As he scurries about, chasing a dropped safety pin, piece of paper or any other object he has found, pick up the object and toss it away from you. As he resumes play with the item, go to where he is playing, pick up the object and toss it a little way away from you again. As he realizes you are playing with him, he will bring the plaything back to you. When he does this, reward him with a tidbit of his favorite food. The pattern of chasing the plaything and bringing it back to you will soon become well established. The object you use should neither be too hard nor too heavy, and make sure it is one for which your cat shows a preference. Don't fool your cat when teaching him this trick. If you go through the motion of throwing the toy for him, then really follow through on it. Deceiving him is a sure way to lose his trust.

Jumping through the hoop is a particularly impressive trick—a miniature version of the big circus cats' flaming hoop trick. This one takes patience and can be said to consist of two

Above: *Mother cats, especially those that give birth outdoors, are very protective and may move the nest several times to keep the young from being located. This instinct harks back to earlier times when such maneuvers were necessary for survival.* **Opposite, upper left:** *This bright-eyed kitten sports a beautiful calico coat.* **Opposite, upper right:** *Cats and dogs can become friends if they are properly introduced from the start.* **Opposite, bottom:** *Be sure to prepare a nest for the pregnant cat to give birth in, and have it ready a few weeks before delivery so she can get used to it.*

different steps. Firstly, make a hoop, possibly out of coat hangers, or a hula hoop works well. Rub food on the hoop and let the cat sniff it. When he decides it is a desirable object, begin your training. Place the hoop upright from, but touching the floor. Holding a piece of food in your hands near the hoop, bring the food nearer and nearer to the direct center of the hoop, giving it to your cat each time he approaches the hoop. Finally, hold the food on the opposite side of the hoop from your cat, making him walk through the hoop in order to reach the food. Now repeat the procedure and each time he goes through the hoop say the word "jump" clearly. After he repeatedly goes through the hoop for the food without hesitation, begin the second step. Lift the hoop off the ground a couple of inches, raising it higher each time the cat goes through. Estimate your cat's capabilities so you never lift the hoop so high it discourages him. Repeat the command "jump" each time he goes through the hoop until he associates the word with the act.

Reward him with tidbits of his favorite food each time he goes through the hoop.

Rolling over is a trick much admired in dogs, but cats do it just as well. Again, have a good supply of food treats on hand to reward your pet with when he has accomplished a step successfully. Tell him to "lie down" and gently push him down and over on his side. Reward him when you have made him lie down this way. When he responds to the "lie down" command you are ready to teach the "roll over" command. Command him to "lie down" and when he has done this, tell him to "roll over," then gently roll him over. Reward him with a treat as soon as you have rolled him over. Repeat this procedure several times, saying the command each time and rewarding him without fail each time he has rolled over with your help. After working with him for a time he will soon do the entire trick from start to finish with just one command, "roll over." Again, the key to successful completion of this trick is gentleness and patience.

Index

Amur Leopard, 15
Bathing, 77
Beds, 32
Bobcat, 11, 20
Burmese cat, 16
Caracal, 20
Cat litters, 50
Cat pans, 50
Chicken, 43
Coat discoloration, 81
Collars, 35
Constipation, 57
Dental care, 73
Diarrhea, 58
Dinictis, 17
Dry cat foods, 43, 76
Dry hair, 80
Ear care, 72
Felis, 20
Fish, 43
Fleas, 57
Golden cats, 20
Hairballs, 55, 62
Handling, 25

Harnesses, 34
Hoplophoneus, 17
Housebreaking, 49
Jaguarundi, 20
Margay, 20
Matting, 62
Miacis, 16
Milk, 41
Nail clipping, 68
Northern Lynx, 11
Ocelot, 11, 14, 20
Organs, 42, 43
Pork, 42
Puma, 20
Scraped food, 41
Scratching pole, 36
Serval, 20
Siamese cat, 9, 12
Stud tail, 64
Toys, 36
Vegetables, 44
Wild cat, 10, 20
Worms, 56

Overleaf: *Sweetness of expression is one of the hallmarks of kittens' charm.*

Kittens
KW-019